Mary Cassatt Self-Portrait

MARY CASSATT

IMPRESSIONIST PAINTER

Young Girl at a Window, by Mary Cassatt

MARY CASSATT

IMPRESSIONIST PAINTER

LOIS V. HARRIS

PELICAN PUBLISHING COMPANY

Gretna 2007

*In memory of my son, Glen Allen Harris, a promising art student (1964-87),
and for my son, James Andrew Harris, with admiration and love*

Many thanks to Pelican Publishing Company for staying afloat and working
on this project in spite of suffering
damage from Hurricane Katrina.

*The word "Pelican" and the depiction of a pelican
are trademarks of Pelican Publishing Company, Inc.,
and are registered in the U.S. Patent and Trademark Office.*

Library of Congress Cataloging-in-Publication Data

Harris, Lois V.
  Mary Cassatt : impressionist painter / Lois V. Harris.
     p. cm.
  ISBN 978-1-58980-452-4 (hardcover : alk. paper)
 1. Cassatt, Mary, 1844-1926—Juvenile literature. 2. Artists—United
States—Biography—Juvenile literature. 3. Impressionism (Art)—Juvenile
literature. I. Cassatt, Mary, 1844-1926. II. Title.
  N6537.C35H37 2007
  759.13—dc22

                                                              2007011755

Printed in Singapore
Published by Pelican Publishing Company, Inc.
1000 Burmaster Street, Gretna, Louisiana 70053

MARY CASSATT

IMPRESSIONIST PAINTER

Young Girl Reading, by Mary Cassatt

When Mary Cassatt was a girl, she dreamed of being a famous painter. But it was 1855 and few artists were women.

Mary was born in 1844 near Pittsburgh, Pennsylvania. When she was seven, her family moved to Europe, where Mary learned French and German. She saw beautiful art in the museums and galleries. In 1855, her family returned to Pennsylvania.

With her parents' encouragement, Mary took drawing lessons. Other girls thought painting was just a hobby, but Mary wanted to sell her paintings and earn her own money.

Mary grew tall and slim. At fifteen, she persuaded her parents to let her go to art school. Most girls waited until they were seventeen or eighteen to do that. Mary rushed to Philadelphia to sign up as a full-time student at the Pennsylvania Academy of the Fine Arts. She was the first in her class to enroll.

The Cassatt children

Pennsylvania Academy of the Fine Arts, 1876

Mary studied art, French, German, and Italian. She was one of the best students. But after two years, Mary thought she could learn faster on her own and went home.

Besides painting, she liked horses and often rode with her brother, Alexander, in the Pennsylvania hills. But she grew restless. She wanted to study art in Europe.

Her father said no at first, but Mary and her mother convinced him to let her go. She was twenty-one. It was 1865, and the Civil War had ended. With her mother, Mary crossed the Atlantic Ocean. She got seasick, and when the ship docked, sailors carried her off.

Mary Cassatt, right, at the Pennsylvania Academy of the Fine Arts

Mary Cassatt at the Louvre, by Edgar Degas

When her mother returned to America, Mary traveled to Spain, Italy, Belgium, and France. In their museums, she copied and learned from the art of the old masters. Mary wanted her paintings to be even better than theirs.

A Session of the Painting Jury at the Salon des Artistes Français, 1883, by Henri Gervex

Judges at the important annual Paris art show, called the Salon, accepted one of Mary's paintings. She was excited. Thousands of people would view her work, and she hoped it sold.

A Woman and a Girl Driving, by Mary Cassatt

Mary moved to Paris, her favorite city. Her friends from art school lived there. They admired her work and encouraged her.

Mary kept her horse in a stable near her apartment. When her family and friends visited, they often went riding in a park.

For the next few years, Mary's paintings sold in the Salon. But she grew tired of painting to please the judges. They made rules and disliked anything new or creative. They liked dark colors and subjects from the past. In the paintings that the judges chose, the people looked stiff and the outdoor scenes seemed unreal.

Mary began using lighter colors. The Salon judges rejected her new paintings. She darkened the colors on one painting, and the next year submitted it. The judges accepted it. Mary's temper exploded. She did not like anyone telling her what to paint.

Spanish Dancer Wearing a Lace Mantilla, by Mary Cassatt

The Ballet Class, by Edgar Degas

In 1875, Mary saw an Edgar Degas painting in an art dealer's window. This painting changed her life. Degas belonged to a group of thirty artists called Impressionists. The Salon judges thought of the Impressionists as a separate group from the rest of the artists. The judges might accept the Impressionists' paintings, but they did not approve of their style. These artists did not follow the judges' rules. The Impressionists used color and light to show ordinary people doing everyday things. They painted what they saw and felt.

Self-portrait, by Edgar Degas

Mary tried the Impressionists' methods and liked this new way of painting. Degas invited her to display her work with the Impressionists rather than in the Salon. Mary believed that artists should be free to create work in their own way, and she joined the group of mostly French painters. She was the only American.

The Impressionists advised and inspired her, especially Degas. The two were good friends for over forty years.

Many of the Impressionists painted outdoors. Mary left her studio and drew people in garden scenes. First, she sketched the poses and settings.

Back in her studio, she posed a model to look like the one in her sketchbook and painted the scene.

Poppies in a Field, by Mary Cassatt

15

Little Girl in a Blue Armchair, by Mary Cassatt

Mary also painted pictures of indoor life. The people in her pictures showed their feelings in their faces.

By mixing the methods of the old masters and the new Impressionists, she came up with her own style.

Girl Arranging Her Hair, by Mary Cassatt

France appreciated Mary Cassatt's art. The government asked her for a painting for the Luxembourg Museum, which was known for its modern art. Her paintings and prints sold in Europe, but she was not well known in America. She persuaded her visiting American friends and relatives to buy the Impressionists' art.

Young Girl Sewing in a Garden, by Mary Cassatt

In 1889, workers finished building the Eiffel Tower. It was the world's tallest manmade structure. From the top, visitors saw all of Paris. Meanwhile, Mary continued to grow as an artist.

The Tea, by Mary Cassatt

Mary learned how to paint skin tones and how to use color,

light, and dark.

In the Loge, by Mary Cassatt

Breakfast in Bed, by Mary Cassatt

Famous for painting loving moments between a mother and child, she never had a child of her own. In Mary's day, most women did not work and raise children at the same time.

Using a soft pastel technique, she painted portraits of her nieces and nephews and her friends' children.

Sailor Boy: Portrait of Gardner Cassatt as a Child, by Mary Cassatt

Mrs. Cassatt Knitting, Profile View, by Mary Cassatt

When the children grew restless from posing, Mary's mother read stories to entertain them. After Mary's father retired, her parents had left America to live with her.

An American critic called Mary's work original and attractive. Other Americans began to admire her paintings, pastels, and prints. Mary was surprised to learn that, after so many years, Americans appreciated her work.

The Banjo Lesson, by Mary Cassatt

25

In 1892, Mary bought a home with her own money in Beaufresne, not far from Paris. She hung the Impressionists' paintings on its walls. In her garden, she planted fruit trees, chrysanthemums, and a thousand rosebushes. She grew American corn, eggplant, and other vegetables. Famous people enjoyed her dinner parties, especially when she served her caramel candy.

Portrait of Alexander J. Cassatt and His Son, Robert Kelso Cassatt, by Mary Cassatt

Mary became a heroine to American art students in Paris. They said she stood for freedom in the arts more than any other American artist of her time. She encouraged and advised these struggling artists. Many of them painted in the Impressionists' style. Mary offered scholarships if students agreed to copy the old masters' work for one year.

In 1904, France presented to Mary Cassatt one of its highest awards, the Chevalier of the Legion of Honor. She proudly wore the red ribbon often.

As Mary aged, her eyesight failed. She endured several eye operations. By 1918, when World War I ended, she could barely see. She stopped painting.

In 1926, Mary died. She was eighty-two. France gave her a grand funeral with military honors. Her neighbors filled the church with roses. American newspapers praised Mary Cassatt as one of the best women painters of all time.

Woman Reading, by Mary Cassatt

Before her death, American museums ignored her art. Afterwards, they acquired her prints, pale pastel drawings, and paintings from private citizens.

Smiling Sara in a Big Hat Holding Her Dog,
by Mary Cassatt

The museums also received from Mary's friends and relatives the Impressionists' artworks that she had helped them select.

Child in a Straw Hat, by Mary Cassatt

Family Group Reading, by Mary Cassatt

When Mary was a girl, she dreamed of becoming a famous painter and earning her own money. She worked hard all her life and achieved more than she ever imagined. By following her own plan, she became one of the world's greatest Impressionist painters.

CREDITS

p. 1: *Mary Cassatt Self-Portrait,* ca. 1880, Mary Stevenson Cassatt, gouache and water-color over graphite on paper, image: 32.7cm x 24.6cm (12⁷/₈" x 9¹¹/₁₆"), sheet: 33.1cm x 24.6cm (13¹/₁₆" x 9¹¹/₁₆"), National Portrait Gallery, Smithsonian Institution, NPG.76.33.

p. 2: *Young Girl at a Window,* 1883-1885, Mary Stevenson Cassatt, oil on canvas, 39¹/₂ x 25¹/₂ inches, Acc.no.: 09.8, In the Collection of The Corcoran Gallery of Art, Washington, DC. Museum Purchase, Gallery Fund.

p. 5: *Young Girl Reading (Jeune Fille Lisant),* ca. 1894, Mary Cassatt, pastel on paper, Hirshhorn Museum and Sculpture Garden, Smithsonian Institution, The Joseph H. Hirshhorn Bequest, 1981. Photograph: Lee Stalsworth.

p. 6 top: *Photograph of a drawing of the Cassatt children by Peter Baumgartner from about 1854.* Image is courtesy of the Frederick A. Sweet research material on Mary Cassatt and James A. McNeill Whistler, 1872-1975, in the Archives of American Art, Smithsonian Institution.

p. 6 bottom: *Pennsylvania Academy of the Fine Arts, 1876,* Frederick Gutekunst, photographer, courtesy of the Pennsylvania Academy of the Fine Arts, Philadelphia. Archives.

p. 7 left: *Mary Cassatt, Eliza Haldeman, Miss Welsh, Inez Lewis, and Dr. Edward Smith casting a hand at the Pennsylvania Academy of the Fine Arts, 1862,* photographer unknown, courtesy of the Pennsylvania Academy of the Fine Arts, Philadelphia. Archives.

p. 7 right: *Mary Cassatt,* 1872, Baroni and Gardelli, photographers, carte di visite, albumen print, courtesy of the Pennsylvania Academy of the Fine Arts, Philadelphia. Archives.

p. 8: *Mary Cassatt at the Louvre: The Etruscan Gallery,* 1879-80, Edgar Degas, French, 1834-1917, soft ground etching, drypoint, aquatint and etching, Catalogue Raisonné: Reed and Shapiro 51, seventh state; Delteil 30, Platemark: 26.7 x 23.2 cm (10¹/₂ x 9¹/₈ in.); Sheet: 42.0 x 31.0 (16⁹/₁₆ x 12³/₁₆ in.), Museum of Fine Arts, Boston, Katherine E. Bullard Fund in memory of Francis Bullard, by exchange, 1983.310. Photograph © 2007 Museum of Fine Arts, Boston.

p. 9: *A Session of the Painting Jury at the Salon des Artistes Français, 1883,* 1885, Henri Gervex, Musée d'Orsay, Paris, France. Photograph © Erich Lessing/Art Resource, NY.

p. 10: *A Woman and a Girl Driving,* 1881, Mary Cassatt, Philadelphia Museum of Art: Purchased with the W. P. Wilstach Fund, 1921.

p. 11: *Spanish Dancer Wearing a Lace Mantilla,* 1873, Mary Cassatt, Smithsonian American Art Museum, Washington, DC, U.S.A. Photograph © Smithsonian American Art Museum, Washington, DC/Art Resource, NY.

p. 12: *The Ballet Class,* ca. 1880, Edgar Degas, Philadelphia Museum of Art: Purchased with the W. P. Wilstach Fund, 1937.

p. 13: *Self-portrait,* ca. 1857-1858, Edgar Degas, oil on paper, laid down on canvas, 20.6 x 15.9 cm (8¹/₈ x 6¹/₄ in.), The J. Paul Getty Museum, Los Angeles.

pp. 14-15: *Poppies in a Field,* Mary Cassatt, Philadelphia Museum of Art: Bequest of Charlotte Dorrance Wright, 1978.

p. 16: *Little Girl in a Blue Armchair,* 1878, Mary Cassatt, oil on canvas, image © 2006 Board of Trustees, National Gallery of Art, Washington. Collection of Mr. and Mrs. Paul Mellon.

p. 17: *Girl Arranging Her Hair,* 1886, Mary Cassatt, oil on canvas, image © 2006 Board of Trustees, National Gallery of Art, Washington. Chester Dale Collection.

p. 18: *Young Girl Sewing in a Garden,* 1880-1882, Mary Cassatt, Musée d'Orsay, Paris, France. Photograph © Erich Lessing/Art Resource, NY.

p. 19: *Aerial View of Paris, France, from Balloon,* 1889, Alphonse Liébert, photographer, photographic print, Library of Congress, Washington, DC.

p. 20: *The Tea,* ca. 1880, Mary Stevenson Cassatt, American, 1844-1926, oil on canvas, 64.77 x 92.07 cm (25¹/₂ x 36¹/₄ in.), Museum of Fine Arts, Boston, M. Theresa B. Hopkins Fund, 42.178. Photograph © 2007 Museum of Fine Arts, Boston.

p. 21: *In the Loge,* 1878, Mary Stevenson Cassatt, American, 1844-1926, oil on canvas, 81.28 x 66.04 cm (32 x 26 in.), Museum of Fine Arts, Boston, The Hayden Collection—Charles Henry Hayden Fund, 10.35. Photograph © 2007 Museum of Fine Arts, Boston.

p. 22: *Breakfast in Bed,* 1897, Mary Cassatt, oil on canvas, 25⁵/₈ x 29", courtesy of the Huntington Library, Art Collections, and Botanical Gardens, San Marino, California.

p. 23: *Sailor Boy: Portrait of Gardner Cassatt as a Child,* 1892, Mary Stevenson Cassatt, pastel on paper, Philadelphia Museum of Art: Gift of Mrs. Gardner Cassatt, 1961.

p. 24: *Mrs. Cassatt Knitting, Profile View,* Mary Stevenson Cassatt, Philadelphia Museum of Art: Purchased with the Joseph E. Temple Fund, 1949.

p. 25: *The Banjo Lesson,* 1894, Mary Cassatt, pastel on paper, 28 x 22¹/₂ in. [71.1 x 52.2 cm.], Virginia Museum of Fine Arts, Richmond. The Adolph D. and Wilkins C. Williams Fund. Photo: Katherine Wetzel, © Virginia Museum of Fine Arts.

p. 26: *Portrait of Alexander J. Cassatt and His Son, Robert Kelso Cassatt,* 1884, Mary Stevenson Cassatt, Philadelphia Museum of Art: Purchased with the W. P. Wilstach Fund and with funds contributed by Mrs. William Coxe Wright, 1959.

p. 27: *Portrait of Mary Cassatt, 1914.* Image is courtesy of the Frederick A. Sweet research material on Mary Cassatt and James A. McNeill Whistler, 1872-1975, in the Archives of American Art, Smithsonian Institution.

p. 28: *Woman Reading (Femme lisant),* 1878-1879, Mary Cassatt, Joslyn Art Museum, Omaha, Nebraska.

p. 29: *Smiling Sara in a Big Hat Holding Her Dog,* ca. 1901, Mary Cassatt, pastel over a pastel counterproof on paper, 27¹/₂ x 22³/₄ in. [69.8 x 57.8 cm.], Acc.no.: 2003.1.1, courtesy of the Pennsylvania Academy of the Fine Arts, Philadelphia. The Vivian O. and Meyer P. Potamkin Collection. Bequest of Vivian O. Potamkin.

p. 30: *Child in a Straw Hat,* ca. 1886, Mary Cassatt, oil on canvas, image © 2006 Board of Trustees, National Gallery of Art, Washington. Collection of Mr. and Mrs. Paul Mellon.

p. 31: *Family Group Reading,* ca. 1901, Mary Stevenson Cassatt, Philadelphia Museum of Art: Gift of Mr. and Mrs. J. Watson Webb, 1942.